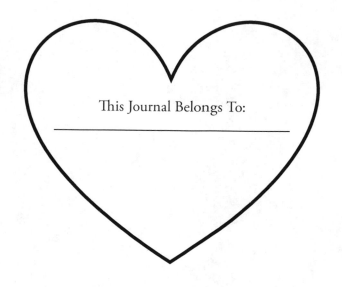

This Journal Belongs To:
_____

# IF ALL WOMEN ARE GOLD DIGGERS

## WHAT ARE MEN?

CRENIQUE

authorHOUSE®

*AuthorHouse*™
*1663 Liberty Drive*
*Bloomington, IN 47403*
*www.authorhouse.com*
*Phone: 1 (800) 839-8640*

*Published by AuthorHouse    12/03/2015*

*ISBN: 978-1-5049-6459-3 (sc)*
*ISBN: 978-1-5049-6458-6 (e)*

# CONTENTS

# 1

# If All Women Are Gold Diggers....... What Are Men?

Men say women are gold diggers. If we are gold diggers then what are men? Coochie diggers. Women want financial security and men want free pussy. Do women really have to go out there in the streets and sell their bodies to get what they want? No. If a woman learned how to be stingy with her pussy just like a man is stingy with his money she will get what she wants. Men need women vaginas to keep them from dating "Palmila". If all women learned how to play the game "Keep that pussy in your pants until that man break bread" they will be some true winners in fair exchange no robbery. I learned the game after I gave my body up to ungrateful grown boys. They took advantage of it and left me with the gynecologist bill. Did they spend money on the period pads monthly? No, I did. Did they buy the hygiene products to keep it fresh? No, I did. Did they pay to have it waxed? No, I did. If a woman takes care of her man that makes her his king and he's her queen because he has feminine ways. Same goes for a man who likes to hit women, he's just mad because he can't be her.

Men want a woman to go to work and make her own money and then, come home and work for him for free. How is she a gold digger? If you want her to work for you that means she should quick her job and be your employee and get paid from you…she's not a gold digger, she's just doing her job. Just like a part-time job, he wants her to be on call…only when he need her. But, in a relationship with a selfish man, she's working for free, as if she's his intern.

Chicken Thigh: A deadbeat father who only comes around when he wants sex from you, not to see his kids. Even though, he's in a relationship with another woman, he still creeps with his baby mama.

Chicken Wing: A deadbeat father who loves to have sex with women and leave them stuck raising his eggs. He flew away because he doesn't want to be a dad. Forgive him, he's not running away from his kids, he's running away from himself. Anytime a father denies his kids, he's actually denying himself, because babies are created by a man, so if he don't love his child, he actually don't love himself. When he denies his child, he is actually denying himself. That child is a reflection of him. He don't know who he is as a man and it's not his fault. He was abused when he was a little boy by his father and now he is trying to figure out how to love himself. Leave him alone, don't interrupt him from learning how to love, he's not a grown man, he's a grown boy with low self-esteem issues.

Chicken Breast: A deadbeat father who acts like he's the child instead of the adult. This grown boy depends on his baby mama for allowance. When he don't get his way, he throws tantrums like a little baby, he will also steal his baby mama car and money and stay gone for weeks, he doesn't care about his kids, he only cares about himself.

Chicken Leg: A deadbeat father who spends more time outside then he do inside with his kids. When he's at home, he doesn't spend time with his kids, he can't sit still long enough to watch a movie with his wife and kids without being bored, he has street feet, hanging out partying with his friends. He spends more time with his friends' then he do with his family. He is still a grown boy.

Cup of Noodle: A man who is content with depending on a woman for a place to live, transportation, food, clothes and money. He's broke and lazy, and don't want to work. His excuse is, he has a bad back, but there isn't anything wrong with him when he's putting his back into sex. He's another bill, he is only worth $0.25. A cheap cup of noodle dude, who will run through you, leaving you hungry. Study a man like he is arithmetic. Always choose the plus sign and the multiply sign as your healthy options. Never be in a relationship with a man who is the minus or the division, he will keep you broke. Anytime you have to divide your money up between you and a man is bad on his end for being a man and depending on you for financial support, and it's bad on your end for being with a man who is using you. Choose your math symbols wisely. He got to bring something to the table. Just know, if you do end up being with this man you will stay broke, hungry and sick from high blood pressure with all the sodium cup of noodles have, he's not healthy for you.

Brussel Sprout: A Brussel sprout is a man who wish he was a woman because he loves to argue with them, he has no problem going head up with a woman. He always plays victim. You will be the one buying him roses instead of him buying you roses because he will be your queen and you will be his king. He is a HESHE, a man who was put in this world to be a king, now he is a queen. Brussels sprouts are Gay boys, they are good friends but not good to sex. They are low-key feminine dudes who bully girls. The food Brussels sprouts are healthy for you to eat, but the human Brussel sprout is bad for you to sex.

Spam: This man is like the internet spam and the food spam, you try to block him out of your life but he keeps showing up, when you breakup with him he's sitting at your front door reading a book, waiting for you to open your door, he's a true stalker and a harasser, no such thing as a restraining order, it won't keep him away. Just like sodium, he is the cause of high blood pressure.

Beef: The bible tells us in Deuteronomy, not to fall in love with this man, yes, it's okay to date the grass-fed cow, but don't marry him, he's not healthy for your heart, he will bring all kinds of health problems into your life and having you sitting at the emergency room wasting money on hospital bills, yes, he's delicious, but he's not good for you. This man knows how to love a woman and break her heart, leaving her fighting for her life because of heart disease, he knows how to make love to a woman but he's physically abusive, he is a tough hearted bully, and very addictive, if a woman loves her life she will breakup with this guy before he kills her.

Pop Tart: This is an artificially sweet man, he will do everything you need him to do, those empty spots he will fill them, those late night cravings, he will heal them, the way he will touch you, will make you feel satisfied, when you need him, he'll be there on time to keep you company. This man is playing the row of a grown man, he will wine-n-dine you with the finer things in life in the beginning of getting to know him, but eleven months later he is breaking up with you after he is tired of putting his pop tart inside your microwavable oven. He will have you believing he is your soulmate, he knows how to provide and protect and guide his temporary woman but, he don't know how to man up and settle down with one woman. He's a good performer but not a good man, he is still a grown boy. Beware, this man will spoil you with luxury things and he will cook for you and treat you like a queen, but that don't mean he loves you, it only means he's a good performer not a good husband.

Bad Sugar: This man loves a woman's outer appearance, he will never fall in love with women who were born with one eye or one leg, he wants his woman to be perfect, but, he will use this woman until he gets on his feet, having her believe he loved her unconditionally, he is the cause of a woman's unhappiness. He is verbally abusive. He will continue to take advantage of her as long as she lets him.

Pig: A selfish businessman who only thinks about himself. He is a guy who will interrupt you from fixing your life. He wants all your time even though he knows that you are busy building your own business. If you meet a man like this, tell him your name is Halloween, he's your trick, you are his treat. He must trick his money on buying you a new life

5

before getting your treat. If he wants you to hang out with him, he got to pay you for all the money you are missing while hanging out with him. Ask him can he afford to buy a HUD home, because you are a Fixer Upper. You need to be fixed up. If he refuses to help you financially, tell him you are busy fixing your life.

Kale: If you want a good Veggie type of man, Kale is the man. When your vision is impaired, kale will be right there, healing your eyes so you can see again. When your lungs can't breathe, kale will bring the magnesium that it need. When your heart is skipping beats, kale will bring the potassium. When your body is aching from the cold or flu and can't sleep, kale will bring the vitamin c for the immune. When your bones are weak, kale will bring the calcium, he is a good man to marry.

Sweet Potato: A naturally sweet man who will love you unconditionally. He will give your vision that beta-carotene faith it needs to let you see how beautiful you are regardless of what people say, he will tell you that your eye is a creative and unique beauty mark. He is healthy and wealthy, he's all about taking care of his woman. He will keep your skin looking soft and healthy.

Carrot: A man who will provide the Vitamin A to help you see. He's the night man who you need when you can't see your haters coming your way at night. He will protect your vision while you drive to your destiny. He is not afraid of commitment, he will put that diamond ring on your finger and marry you.

Blueberry: A man who will provide the Antioxidants to keep cancer from attacking your body. He's also that brain power to keep you smart and thinking intelligently. When you can't find your keys, he will remind you where you placed them. When you need help with homework in college, he will make sure your brain is full of knowledge.

King Salmon: He's the man who chicken, beef and pig wish they were, a grown man. He's living the life that those men wish they lived, wealthy. He romances his lady and spoils her with the luxury life. King Salmon is worth a lot of money, he is a good performer and a grown man. He is a fitness and registered dietician nutritionist, he got that protein you need to tone those muscles. He is the doctor you need to keep your brain and your heart healthy with his omega-3-fatty acids.

Bamboo: A man who is healthier than wood, he'll kick those polluted freeloaders out of your home so you can live a healthier life. You can learn a lot from Mr. Bamboo, he'll teach you how to ignore your haters, keep your head up looking unbothered, and be unbreakable. Every woman wish they had him in their life. He'll build you that dream home, and he'll custom make your furniture and floors. He'll lay you on the bed, and the floor, or he'll sit you on the sofa, and countertop, or hold you up against the wall, and sex you right. He'll teach you how to speak up and be heard, he's that Eco-Friendly Green you need to be happy, healthy, and at peace.

Lemon: When you are vomiting every night, and your fever is very high, lemon will be there, in a heartbeat to heal your life. He will remove every toxic dude that tried to kill you.

Garlic: He is the man that all bad men wish to be, he will kill all those diseased men who left their parasites inside of you, when your blood pressure is high, he will get it back right, when your lungs has fungus, he is the natural antibiotic you need.

Onion: Just like Lemon and Garlic, he will kill those toxic men who are trying to hurt you. If you are about that life, you should make love to all three men for healthier sex, every day, for your morning tea, and at night before you go to sleep, they will do your body right. Onion will run that mucus out of your lungs so you can breathe.

Tobacco: This man is very abusive, he will choke you out and have you waking up in the hospital with low oxygen from an asthma attack. He is bad for your health.

Cocaine: This man is mentally ill, and he will mentally, emotionally, and financially drain you dry. He is bad for your wealth.

Heart: This man is jealous of the relationship you have with your dad, he will destroy your father and daughter relationship by keeping you away from your dad. He is mentally and physically unhealthy. He tells you that he loves you, but he doesn't love himself because he smokes cigarettes.

Diamond: A hustler who knows how to hustle a woman out of her money. He hangs out in Beverly Hills at the jewelry store looking for his victims to hustle them out of their money. Wherever your money goes, he goes. He envies your income level, he doesn't want his woman to outshine him. So, he'll use his best persuasive game to get you to break bread with him.

Club: A player is an actor who knows how to play the role of a good man. He will take advantage you, he will bring another woman into your home, in your bed and cheat on you. He will drive another woman around in your car. He won't protect you even if you were his wife, because he don't care about your life. This guy is also at the strip clubs and at the after hour clubs, looking for some after hour pussy, he treats you how you carry yourself, if you carry yourself like a club hopper, he will hop on your pussy because he's a pussy hopper, and after he is tired of dancing inside of you, he will move on to the next.

Rock: This man's mental and physical health is solid rock, you won't hear no weakness come out of his mouth, because he is too strong to be a victim. He will keep you mentally, emotionally and physically strong. He won't let you give up on you. He won't control you. His job is to make sure you stay healthy. He's your mental and physical doctor. He will guide you to good health.

Paper: A man who will be there financially when you need him. He's the provider not the divider. He's too grown to complain about a woman not having her own. As long as this multibillionaire is wealthy your pocketbook is filled. He will provide you with wealth.

Scissors: A man who will have your back when another man disrespects you. He will protect you.

# 2

# Chicken Thigh

Have you ever been in a relationship with Chicken Thigh? If so, how did he make you feel?

_____

_____

_____

_____

_____

_____

_____

_____

_____

_____

_____

_____

_____

_____

_____

_____

_____

_____

*Crenique*

_____

_____

_____

_____

_____

_____

_____

_____

_____

_____

_____

_____

_____

_____

_____

_____

_____

_____

_____

_____

_____

_____

_____

_____

_____

_____

_____

_____

_____

_____

_____

_____

_____

_____

_____

_____

_____

_____

_____

_____

_____

_____

_____

_____

_____

_____

_____

_____

_____

_____

_____

_____

_____

_____

_____

*Crenique*

# 3

# Chicken Wing

Have you ever been in a relationship with Chicken Wing? If so, how did he make you feel?

_____

_____

_____

_____

_____

_____

_____

_____

_____

_____

_____

_____

_____

_____

_____

_____

_____

_____

_____

*Crenique*

_____

_____

_____

_____

_____

_____

_____

_____

_____

_____

_____

_____

_____

_____

_____

_____

_____

_____

_____

_____

_____

_____

_____

_____

_____

_____

_____

_____

*Crenique*

# 4

# Chicken Breast

Have you ever been in a relationship with Chicken Breast? If so, how did he make you feel?

_____

_____

_____

_____

_____

_____

_____

_____

_____

_____

_____

_____

_____

_____

_____

_____

*Crenique*

*Crenique*

# 5

# Chicken Leg

Have you ever been in a relationship with Chicken Leg? If so, how did he make you feel?

_____

_____

_____

_____

_____

_____

_____

_____

_____

_____

_____

_____

_____

_____

_____

_____

_____

_____

_____

*Crenique*

_____

_____

_____

_____

_____

_____

_____

_____

_____

_____

_____

_____

_____

_____

_____

_____

_____

_____

_____

_____

_____

_____

_____

_____

_____

_____

_____

_____

*Crenique*

# 6

# Cup of Noodles

Have you ever been in a relationship with Cup of Noodles? If so, how did he make you feel?

_____

_____

_____

_____

_____

_____

_____

_____

_____

_____

_____

_____

_____

_____

_____

_____

_____

*Crenique*

_____

_____

_____

_____

_____

_____

_____

_____

_____

_____

_____

_____

_____

_____

_____

_____

_____

_____

_____

_____

_____

_____

_____

_____

_____

_____

_____

_____

_____

_____

*Crenique*

# 7

# Brussel Sprout

Have you ever been in a relationship with Brussel Sprout? If so, how did he make you feel?

_____

_____

_____

_____

_____

_____

_____

_____

_____

_____

_____

_____

_____

_____

_____

_____

_____

*Crenique*

_____
_____
_____
_____
_____
_____
_____
_____
_____
_____
_____
_____
_____
_____
_____
_____
_____
_____
_____
_____
_____
_____
_____
_____
_____
_____

*Crenique*

# 8

# Spam

Have you ever been in a relationship with Spam? If so, how did he make you feel?

_____

_____

_____

_____

_____

_____

_____

_____

_____

_____

_____

_____

_____

_____

_____

_____

*Crenique*

*Crenique*

_____

_____

_____

_____

_____

_____

_____

_____

_____

_____

_____

_____

_____

_____

_____

_____

_____

_____

_____

_____

_____

_____

_____

_____

_____

_____

_____

# 9

# Beef

Have you ever been in a relationship with Beef? If so, how did he make you feel?

_____

_____

_____

_____

_____

_____

_____

_____

_____

_____

_____

_____

_____

_____

_____

_____

_____

*Crenique*

_____
_____
_____
_____
_____
_____
_____
_____
_____
_____
_____
_____
_____
_____
_____
_____
_____
_____
_____
_____
_____
_____
_____
_____
_____
_____
_____
_____

_____

_____

_____

_____

_____

_____

_____

_____

_____

_____

_____

_____

_____

_____

_____

_____

_____

_____

_____

_____

_____

_____

_____

_____

_____

_____

_____

_____

_____

*Crenique*

_____
_____
_____
_____
_____
_____
_____
_____
_____
_____
_____
_____
_____
_____
_____
_____
_____
_____
_____
_____
_____
_____
_____
_____
_____
_____
_____
_____
_____

# 10

# Pot Tart

Have you ever been in a relationship with Pop Tart? If so, how did he make you feel?

_____

_____

_____

_____

_____

_____

_____

_____

_____

_____

_____

_____

_____

_____

_____

_____

*Crenique*

*Crenique*

# 11

# Bad Sugar

Have you ever been in a relationship with Bad Sugar? If so, how did he make you feel?

_____

_____

_____

_____

_____

_____

_____

_____

_____

_____

_____

_____

_____

_____

_____

_____

_____

_____

*Crenique*

_____

_____

_____

_____

_____

_____

_____

_____

_____

_____

_____

_____

_____

_____

_____

_____

_____

_____

_____

_____

_____

_____

_____

_____

_____

_____

_____

_____

_____

_____

*Crenique*

_____
_____
_____
_____
_____
_____
_____
_____
_____
_____
_____
_____
_____
_____
_____
_____
_____
_____
_____
_____
_____
_____
_____
_____
_____
_____

# 12

# Pig

Have you ever been in a relationship with Pig? If so, how did he make you feel?

_____

_____

_____

_____

_____

_____

_____

_____

_____

_____

_____

_____

_____

_____

_____

_____

_____

_____

*Crenique*

_____

_____

_____

_____

_____

_____

_____

_____

_____

_____

_____

_____

_____

_____

_____

_____

_____

_____

_____

_____

_____

_____

_____

_____

_____

_____

_____

_____

_____

*Crenique*

# 13

# Kale

Have you ever been in a relationship with Kale? If so, how did he make you feel?

_____

_____

_____

_____

_____

_____

_____

_____

_____

_____

_____

_____

_____

_____

_____

_____

_____

*Crenique*

_____
_____
_____
_____
_____
_____
_____
_____
_____
_____
_____
_____
_____
_____
_____
_____
_____
_____
_____
_____
_____
_____
_____
_____
_____

*Crenique*

# 14

# Sweet Potato

Have you ever been in a relationship with Sweet Potato? If so, how did he make you feel?

_____

_____

_____

_____

_____

_____

_____

_____

_____

_____

_____

_____

_____

_____

_____

_____

_____

*Crenique*

*Crenique*

_____

_____

_____

_____

_____

_____

_____

_____

_____

_____

_____

_____

_____

_____

_____

_____

_____

_____

_____

_____

_____

_____

_____

_____

_____

_____

# 15

# King Salmon

Have you ever been in a relationship with King Salmon? If so, how did he make you feel?

_____

_____

_____

_____

_____

_____

_____

_____

_____

_____

_____

_____

_____

_____

_____

_____

_____

*Crenique*

*Crenique*

_____

_____

_____

_____

_____

_____

_____

_____

_____

_____

_____

_____

_____

_____

_____

_____

_____

_____

_____

_____

_____

_____

_____

_____

_____

_____

_____

# 16

# Lemon

Have you ever been in a relationship with Lemon? If so, how did he make you feel?

_____

_____

_____

_____

_____

_____

_____

_____

_____

_____

_____

_____

_____

_____

_____

_____

_____

_____

*Crenique*

_____
_____
_____
_____
_____
_____
_____
_____
_____
_____
_____
_____
_____
_____
_____
_____
_____
_____
_____
_____
_____
_____
_____
_____
_____
_____
_____

*Crenique*

# 17

# Garlic

Have you ever been in a relationship with Garlic? If so, how did he make you feel?

_____

_____

_____

_____

_____

_____

_____

_____

_____

_____

_____

_____

_____

_____

_____

_____

_____

*Crenique*

*Crenique*

# 18

# Onion

Have you ever been in a relationship with Onion? If so, how did he make you feel?

_____

_____

_____

_____

_____

_____

_____

_____

_____

_____

_____

_____

_____

_____

_____

_____

*Crenique*

_____

_____

_____

_____

_____

_____

_____

_____

_____

_____

_____

_____

_____

_____

_____

_____

_____

_____

_____

_____

_____

_____

_____

_____

_____

_____

_____

_____

_____

_____

_____

_____

_____

_____

_____

_____

_____

_____

_____

_____

_____

_____

_____

_____

_____

_____

_____

_____

_____

_____

_____

_____

_____

_____

_____

_____

*Crenique*

# 19

# Tobacco

Have you ever been in a relationship with Tobacco? If so, how did he make you feel?

_____

_____

_____

_____

_____

_____

_____

_____

_____

_____

_____

_____

_____

_____

_____

_____

_____

_____

*Crenique*

# 20

# Cocaine

Have you ever been in a relationship with Cocaine? If so, how did he make you feel?

_____

_____

_____

_____

_____

_____

_____

_____

_____

_____

_____

_____

_____

_____

_____

_____

_____

*Crenique*

_____
_____
_____
_____
_____
_____
_____
_____
_____
_____
_____
_____
_____
_____
_____
_____
_____
_____
_____
_____
_____
_____
_____
_____
_____
_____
_____
_____
_____
_____
_____

*Crenique*

# 21

# Heart

Have you ever been in a relationship with Heart? If so, how did he make you feel?

_____

_____

_____

_____

_____

_____

_____

_____

_____

_____

_____

_____

_____

_____

_____

_____

*Crenique*

*Crenique*

_____

_____

_____

_____

_____

_____

_____

_____

_____

_____

_____

_____

_____

_____

_____

_____

_____

_____

_____

_____

_____

_____

_____

_____

# 22

# Diamond

Have you ever been in a relationship with Diamond? If so, how did he make you feel?

_____

_____

_____

_____

_____

_____

_____

_____

_____

_____

_____

_____

_____

_____

_____

_____

*Crenique*

*Crenique*

_____

_____

_____

_____

_____

_____

_____

_____

_____

_____

_____

_____

_____

_____

_____

_____

_____

_____

_____

_____

_____

_____

_____

_____

_____

# 23

# Club

Have you ever been in a relationship with Club? If so, how did he make you feel?

_____

_____

_____

_____

_____

_____

_____

_____

_____

_____

_____

_____

_____

_____

_____

_____

*Crenique*

*Crenique*

# 24

# Rock

Have you ever been in a relationship with Rock? If so, how did he make you feel?

_____

_____

_____

_____

_____

_____

_____

_____

_____

_____

_____

_____

_____

_____

_____

_____

_____

*Crenique*

*Crenique*

# 25

# Paper

Have you ever been in a relationship with Paper? If so, how did he make you feel?

_____

_____

_____

_____

_____

_____

_____

_____

_____

_____

_____

_____

_____

_____

_____

*Crenique*

*Crenique*

# 26

# Scissors

Have you ever been in a relationship with Scissors? If so, how did he make you feel?

_____

_____

_____

_____

_____

_____

_____

_____

_____

_____

_____

_____

_____

_____

_____

_____

_____

_____

*Crenique*

*Crenique*

# 27

# What Type of Man Will You Marry?

**Man number 1: Chicken**

**Man number 2: Cup of Noodle**

**Man number 3: Pop Tart**

**Man number 4: King Salmon**

**Which one of these men did you choose?** _____
_____

**Why did you choose that type of man?**

_____
_____
_____
_____
_____
_____
_____
_____
_____

*Crenique*

# 28

# Where Will Your Honeymoon Be?

1. In the Alley on Skid Row in Downtown Los Angeles, using a shopping basket for your candlelight dinner.
2. A candlelight dinner inside the pawnshop in San Bernardino, California, with your child crying, saying he or she is hungry while watching you and your man eat.
3. You and your man decided to keep your honeymoon at home and Netflix and Chill to save money to buy your man that brand new video game system he wanted, being that you take care of him financially.
4. Your man decided to take you on a shopping spree in Beverly Hills, California, and fly you to Secrets Resorts in Montego Bay, Jamaica.

**Which one did you choose?** _____
_____

**Why did you choose that location for your honeymoon?**

_____
_____
_____
_____

*Crenique*

# 29

# Where Will You and Your Husband Live?

1. Apartment in San Bernardino, CA.
2. Street in Downtown Los Angeles, CA.
3. House in Victorville, CA.
4. Mansion in Beverly Hills, CA.

**Which one did you choose?** _____

_____

**Why did you choose that place?**

_____

_____

_____

_____

_____

_____

_____

_____

_____

_____

_____

*Crenique*

# 30

# What Is the Source of Income?

1. **Government Assistance:** You are on food stamps and Cash Aid for your one child, and your husband gets a General Relief (GR) check. You get $389 in cash and $195 in food stamps for one child, from Los Angeles, CA. Your man gets $200 in cash and $195 in food stamps from Los Angeles, CA.

2. **J.O.B:** Flipping Burgers for $10 an hour. Your paycheck goes Just On Bills (J.O.B). Your man makes $0.

3. **Career:** Finance Advisor. You make $124,000 a year, but you are always broke because your man is a bill.

4. **Self-Made Billionaires:** You and your husband went to school to learn how to start a business. You sleep or chill on vacation while your residual income makes money for you.

**Which one did you choose?** _____

_____

# Why did you choose that income?

_____
_____
_____
_____
_____
_____
_____
_____
_____
_____
_____
_____
_____
_____
_____
_____
_____
_____
_____
_____
_____
_____
_____
_____
_____
_____

# 31

# What Type of Transportation Will You Have?

1. Bike
2. Bus
3. 10 year old BMW
4. Rolls Royce and a Private Jet

**Which one did you choose?**_____
_____

**Why did you choose it?**

_____
_____
_____
_____
_____
_____
_____
_____
_____
_____

# 32

# What Type of Baby Daddy Will He Be?

1. Chicken Thigh
2. Chicken Wing
3. Chicken Breast
4. Chicken Leg
5. King Salmon

**Which one did you choose?** _____

_____

**Why did you choose that baby daddy?**

_____

_____

_____

_____

_____

_____

_____

_____

_____

_____

*Crenique*

# 33

# How Many Kids Will You Have?

1.  1
2.  3
3.  5
4.  12

**Which one did you choose?** _____

_____

**Why did you choose that many kids?**

_____

_____

_____

_____

_____

_____

_____

_____

_____

_____

_____

_____

_____

_____

_____

_____

_____

_____

_____

_____

_____

_____

**Can you afford to take care of them mentally, emotionally, and financially?**_____

**Are you mentally, emotionally and financially stable?**
_____

**Will you be able to protect your child from child molesters?** _____

**How?**

_____

_____

_____

_____

_____

_____

_____

_____
_____
_____
_____
_____
_____
_____
_____
_____
_____
_____
_____
_____
_____
_____
_____
_____
_____
_____
_____
_____
_____
_____
_____
_____
_____
_____
_____
_____
_____
_____

*Crenique*

# 34

# What Type of Lungs Will You and Your Husband Have?

1. Smokers Lungs
2. Nonsmokers Lungs

**Which one did you choose?** _____

**Why did you choose that one?**

_____

_____

_____

_____

_____

_____

_____

_____

_____

_____

_____

_____

_____

_____

_____

_____

_____

_____

_____

_____

_____

_____

_____

_____

_____

_____

_____

_____

_____

_____

_____

_____

Did you know that drugs, such as cigarettes, marijuana, alcohol, cocaine, PCP, Crystal Meth, Heroin, Opium, Hashish, Amphetamine, Ecstasy, Molly, Speed and LSD are bad for your health? _____

**What are your feelings towards people who do drugs?**

_____

_____

_____

_____

_____

_____

_____

_____

_____

_____

_____

_____

_____

_____

_____

_____

_____

_____

_____

_____

_____

_____

_____

_____

_____

# 35

# What Type of Father Do You Have?

1. Chicken Thigh
2. Chicken Wing
3. Chicken Breast
4. Chicken Leg
5. King Salmon

**Which one did you choose?** _____

**What type of relationship do you have with your dad?**

_____

_____

_____

_____

_____

_____

_____

_____

_____

_____

_____

*Crenique*

*Crenique*

# 36

# Winter

## What Type of Man Will You Marry?

1. _____
2. _____
3. _____
4. _____

## What Color Will Your Wedding Be?

1. _____
2. _____
3. _____
4. _____

## How Many Guests Will You Have?

1. _____
2. _____
3. _____
4. _____

## Where Will Your Honeymoon Be?

1. _____
2. _____
3. _____
4. _____

## How Many Kids Will You Have?

1. _____
2. _____
3. _____
4. _____

## Where Will You Live?

1. _____
2. _____
3. _____
4. _____

## What Will Be Your Source of Income?

1. _____
2. _____
3. _____
4. _____

## What is Your Winter Love Story With Your Husband?:

_____
_____
_____

*Crenique*

*Crenique*

# 37

# Spring

## What type of Man Will You Marry?

1. _____
2. _____
3. _____
4. _____

## What Color Will Your Wedding Be?

1. _____
2. _____
3. _____
4. _____

## How Many Guests Will You Have?

1. _____
2. _____
3. _____
4. _____

## <u>Where Will Your Honeymoon Be?</u>

1. _____
2. _____
3. _____
4. _____

## <u>How Many Kids Will You Have?</u>

1. _____
2. _____
3. _____
4. _____

## <u>Where Will You Live?</u>

1. _____
2. _____
3. _____
4. _____

## <u>What Will Be Your Source of Income?</u>

1. _____
2. _____
3. _____
4. _____

## What is your Spring Love Story with Your Husband?:

_____
_____
_____

*Crenique*

*Crenique*

# 38

# Summer

## What Type of Man Will You Marry?

1. _____
2. _____
3. _____
4. _____

## What Color Will Your Wedding Be?

1. _____
2. _____
3. _____
4. _____

## How Many Guests Will You Have?

1. _____
2. _____
3. _____
4. _____

## **Where will Your Honeymoon Be?**

1. _____
2. _____
3. _____
4. _____

## **How Many Kids Will You Have?**

1. _____
2. _____
3. _____
4. _____

## **Where Will You Live?**

1. _____
2. _____
3. _____
4. _____

## **What Will Be Your Source of Income?**

1. _____
2. _____
3. _____
4. _____

## **What is Your Summer Love Story with Your Husband?:**

_____
_____
_____

*Crenique*

*Crenique*

# 39

# Fall

## What Type of Man Will You Marry?

1. _____
2. _____
3. _____
4. _____

## What Color Will Your Wedding Be?

1. _____
2. _____
3. _____
4. _____

## How Many Guests Will You Have?

1. _____
2. _____
3. _____
4. _____

## Where Will Your Honeymoon Be?

1. _____
2. _____
3. _____
4. _____

## How Many Kids Will You Have?

1. _____
2. _____
3. _____
4. _____

## Where Will You Live?

1. _____
2. _____
3. _____
4. _____

## What Will Be Your Source of Income?

1. _____
2. _____
3. _____
4. _____

## What is Your Fall Love Story with Your Husband?:

_____
_____

_____

*Crenique*

*Crenique*

Printed in the United States
By Bookmasters